KS2 Times Tables

Simon Greaves and Helen Greaves

Contents

Notes to Parents

About this book

This book is full of activities to make times tables practice fun, interesting and challenging for your child. It provides revision of the tables learnt in Key Stage 1 and extensive coverage of the times tables learnt at the start of Key Stage 2. Each table is covered individually and there are reinforcement revision sections throughout the book.

A wide variety of questions, problems and puzzles will enable your child to answer multiplications in a mixture of contexts, enhancing their understanding and ability to rapidly recall basic multiplication facts, one of the essential foundations for good numeracy skills. This book has been compiled by experienced teachers of this age group and supports the National Numeracy Strategy. It will actively encourage home learning and reinforce the skills your child has acquired at school.

How this book will help

- Extensive practice of the six, seven, eight and nine times tables and revision of the three, four, two, five and ten times tables.
- Useful hints and information tips will help your child to identify patterns and learn key multiplication skills.
- Full answers provided at the back of the book.

Published by HarperCollins*Publishers* Ltd
77–85 Fulham Palace Road
London W6 8JB

www.collinseducation.com

© Simon Greaves and Helen Greaves 2004

First published 2004

10 9 8 7 6 5 4 3 2 1

ISBN 0 00 718121 3

The authors assert the moral right to be identified as the authors of this work.

British Library Cataloguing in Publication Data
A catalogue record for this book is available from the British Library.

Written by Simon Greaves and Helen Greaves
Design by Graham M Brasnett
Illustrations by Graham Smith
Cover design by Susi Martin-Taylor
Printed by Printing Express, Hong Kong

Three Times Table

Can you remember?

You should already know these multiplication facts.

Fill in the missing numbers for the three times table.

1	×	3	=	☐
2	×	3	=	☐
3	×	3	=	☐
4	×	3	=	☐
5	×	3	=	☐
6	×	3	=	☐
7	×	3	=	☐
8	×	3	=	☐
9	×	3	=	☐
10	×	3	=	☐

Multiplication maze

Find a path through the maze. You can only go through answers to the three times table.

FINISH

18   26   21   3
7
13   29
30
6   12
4   14   27
25
19   23
15
11   24

START

Buying books

A book costs £3.

How much would it cost to buy:

4 books £ ☐   2 books £ ☐

5 books £ ☐   8 books £ ☐

10 books £ ☐   7 books £ ☐

How many books can you buy for £18? ☐

Mountains
JUNGLE SURVIVAL
£3
Big Adventure
EXPLORING

Well done! Give yourself a star! ⭐

×3 ×3 ×3 ×3 ×3 ×3 ×3 ×3 ×3 ×3 ×3 ×3

Multiplication match

In each line circle the multiplication that matches
the number in the star.

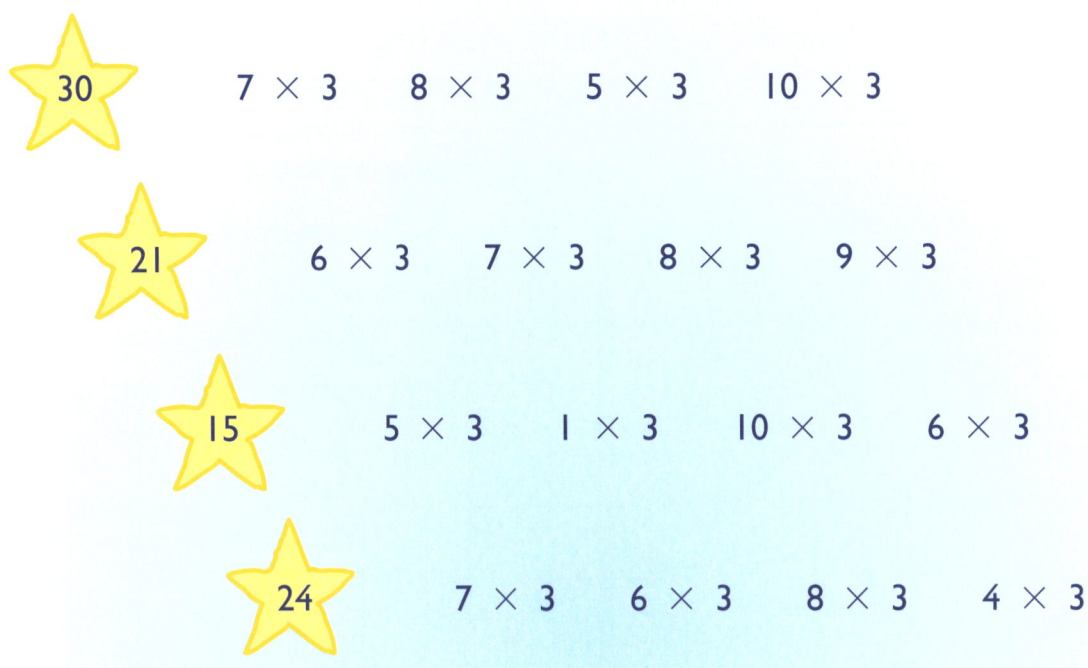

30   7 × 3   8 × 3   5 × 3   10 × 3

21   6 × 3   7 × 3   8 × 3   9 × 3

15   5 × 3   1 × 3   10 × 3   6 × 3

24   7 × 3   6 × 3   8 × 3   4 × 3

Machine madness!

Here is a number machine. Every number that goes into the
machine is multiplied by three.

Fill in the missing numbers.

× 3

☐ ➡ ➡   ➡ ➡ 9

☐ ➡ ➡   ➡ ➡ 24

☐ ➡ ➡   ➡ ➡ 3

☐ ➡ ➡   ➡ ➡ 18

Well done! Give yourself a star!

Four Times Table

Can you remember?

You should already know these multiplication facts.

Fill in the missing numbers for the four times table.

1 × 4 = ☐

2 × 4 = ☐

3 × 4 = ☐

4 × 4 = ☐

5 × 4 = ☐

6 × 4 = ☐

7 × 4 = ☐

8 × 4 = ☐

9 × 4 = ☐

10 × 4 = ☐

Secret shapes

Colour in every shape which contains an answer to the four times table.

What do you see?

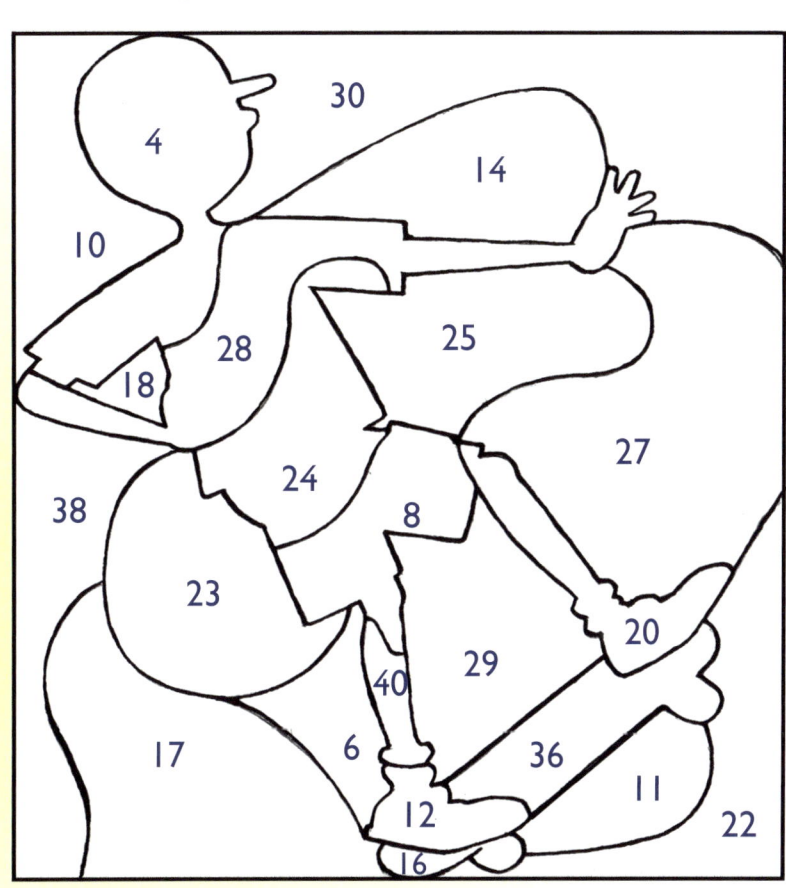

Fairground fun!

A roller coaster ticket costs £4.

How much would it cost to buy:

5 tickets £☐  3 tickets £☐

7 tickets £☐  2 tickets £☐

6 tickets £☐ 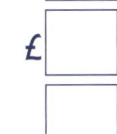 10 tickets £☐

How many tickets can you buy for £16? ☐

Well done! Give yourself a star!

Machine madness!

Here is a number machine. Every number that goes into the machine is doubled and then doubled again.

Write in the missing numbers.

2 → **Double** → **Double** → ☐

4 → → ☐

7 → → ☐

Here is another number machine. Every number that goes into this machine is multiplied by four.

Write in the missing numbers.

2 → **× 4** → ☐

4 → → ☐

7 → → ☐

Look at the numbers the machines are producing. What do you notice about them?

☐

Number path

Here is a grid of numbers.

Colour a path which only goes through answers to the four times table.

1	13	23	34	6	20	→ Finish
3	32	40	36	8	4	
24	28	15	29	18	11	
12	27	5	7	9	38	
16	22	17	14	19	25	

Start →

Well done! Give yourself a star!

Mixed Tables

Money multiplication

Write a multiplication to show the amount of money in each purse.

4 × 5p = 20p

___ × ___ p = ___ p

___ × ___ p = ___ p

___ × ___ p = ___ p

___ × ___ p = ___ p

___ × ___ p = ___ p

Circling sums

Look at these numbers:

16	8	3	15	11	5	20	10	14

Put a **purple** circle around the numbers which are answers in the **two** times table.

Put a **green** circle around the numbers which are answers in the **five** times table.

Put a **yellow** circle around the numbers which are answers in the **ten** times table.

Which numbers have three different coloured rings around them? ☐ and ☐

Which numbers do not have any rings around them? ☐ and ☐

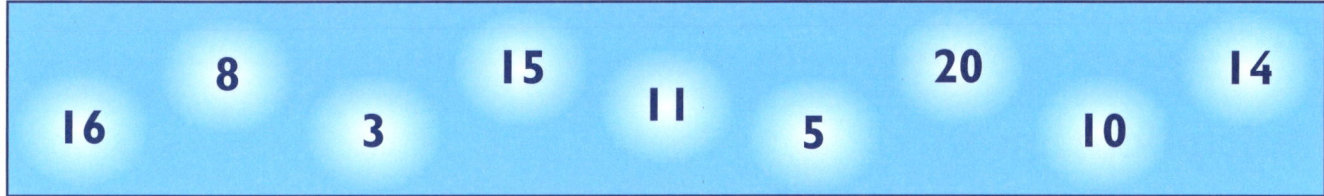

Well done! Give yourself a star!

Machine madness!

Here is a number machine. Every number that goes into the machine is first multiplied by 2 and then by 5.

Write in the missing numbers.

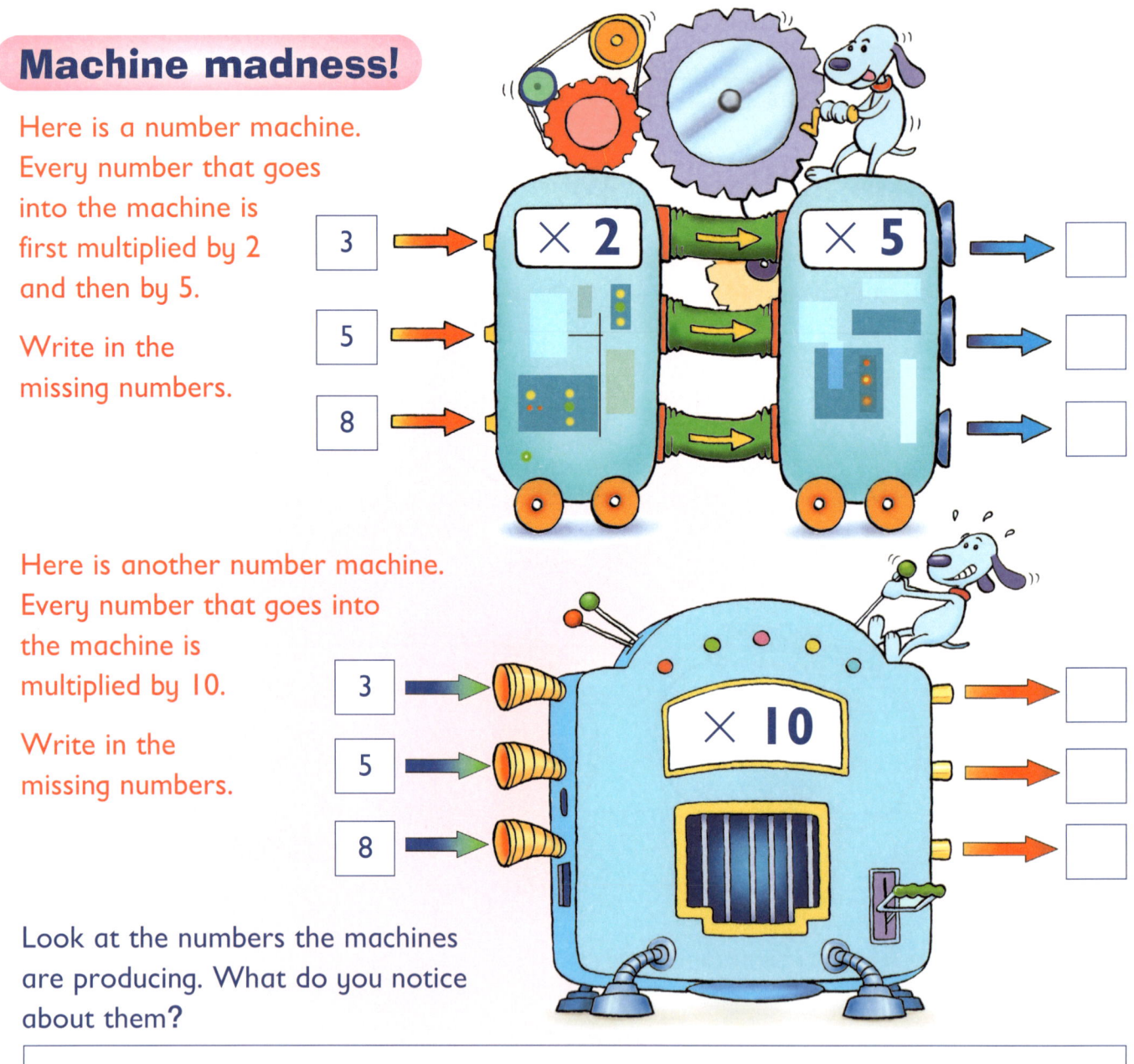

Here is another number machine. Every number that goes into the machine is multiplied by 10.

Write in the missing numbers.

Look at the numbers the machines are producing. What do you notice about them?

Multiplication mix

You should already know these multiplication facts. Here are some questions to test you.

4 × 2 =

5 × 5 =

5 × 10 =

2 × 5 =

7 × 2 =

3 × 5 =

1 × 10 =

9 × 2 =

8 × 2 =

9 × 5 =

10 × 10 =

8 × 10 =

Well done! Give yourself a star!

Six Times Table

What's missing?

Fill in the missing numbers for the six times table.

1	×	6	=	6
2	×	6	=	12
3	×	6	=	☐
☐	×	6	=	24
5	×	6	=	30
6	×	6	=	☐
☐	×	6	=	42
8	×	6	=	48
9	×	6	=	☐
10	×	6	=	60

Let's go shopping!

Here are some clothes for sale in a shop.

£3 £4 £8 £7 £1

How much are six caps? £ ☐

How much are six t-shirts? £ ☐

How much are six jumpers? £ ☐

How much are six pairs of of socks? £ ☐

How much are six pairs of jeans? £ ☐

You can work out the **six** times table if you already know the **three** times table.

1 × 3 = 3	1 × 6 = 6
2 × 3 = 6	2 × 6 = 12
3 × 3 = 9	3 × 6 = 18
4 × 3 = 12	4 × 6 = 24
5 × 3 = 15	5 × 6 = 30
6 × 3 = 18	6 × 6 = 36
7 × 3 = 21	7 × 6 = 42
8 × 3 = 24	8 × 6 = 48
9 × 3 = 27	9 × 6 = 54
10 × 3 = 30	10 × 6 = 60

Each answer in the six times table is **double** that in the three times table.

Well done! Give yourself a star!

Mysterious match!

Draw a line to match each key to its door.

4×6

9×6

3×6

10×6

2×6

7×6

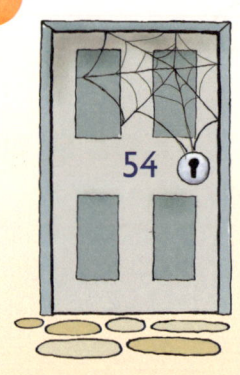 54 24

 18

60

42 12

Machine madness!

Here is a number machine. Every number that goes into the machine is multiplied by six.

Fill in the missing numbers.

6

9

× 6

18

6

24

Well done! Give yourself a star!

Sums for sixes

Here are the answers to the six times table.

Write in the missing numbers.

48	=	☐	×	6		24	=	☐	×	6
42	=	☐	×	6		60	=	☐	×	6
6	=	☐	×	6		12	=	☐	×	6
18	=	☐	×	6		36	=	☐	×	6
54	=	☐	×	6		30	=	☐	×	6

Tricky treasure!

A treasure chest holds six bars of gold.

Write a multiplication to show the number of gold bars in each treasure chest.

3 × 6 = 18

☐ × ☐ = ☐

☐ × ☐ = ☐

☐ × ☐ = ☐

☐ × ☐ = ☐

☐ × ☐ = ☐

Secret sums

Choose the correct answer for each multiplication question. Colour the letter next to that answer.

To find the **product** of two numbers you multiply them together.

5	×	6	=	34	t	or	30	s	
7	×	6	=	42	i	or	44	w	
1	×	6	=	6	n	or	1	e	
2	×	6	=	18	l	or	12	r	
8	×	6	=	54	v	or	48	a	
10	×	6	=	60	m	or	30	e	

The letters that you have **not** coloured spell out the name of a number.

What is the number?

This number is the product of which multiplication in the six times table?

Number path

Find a path through the maze which only goes through answers in the six times table.

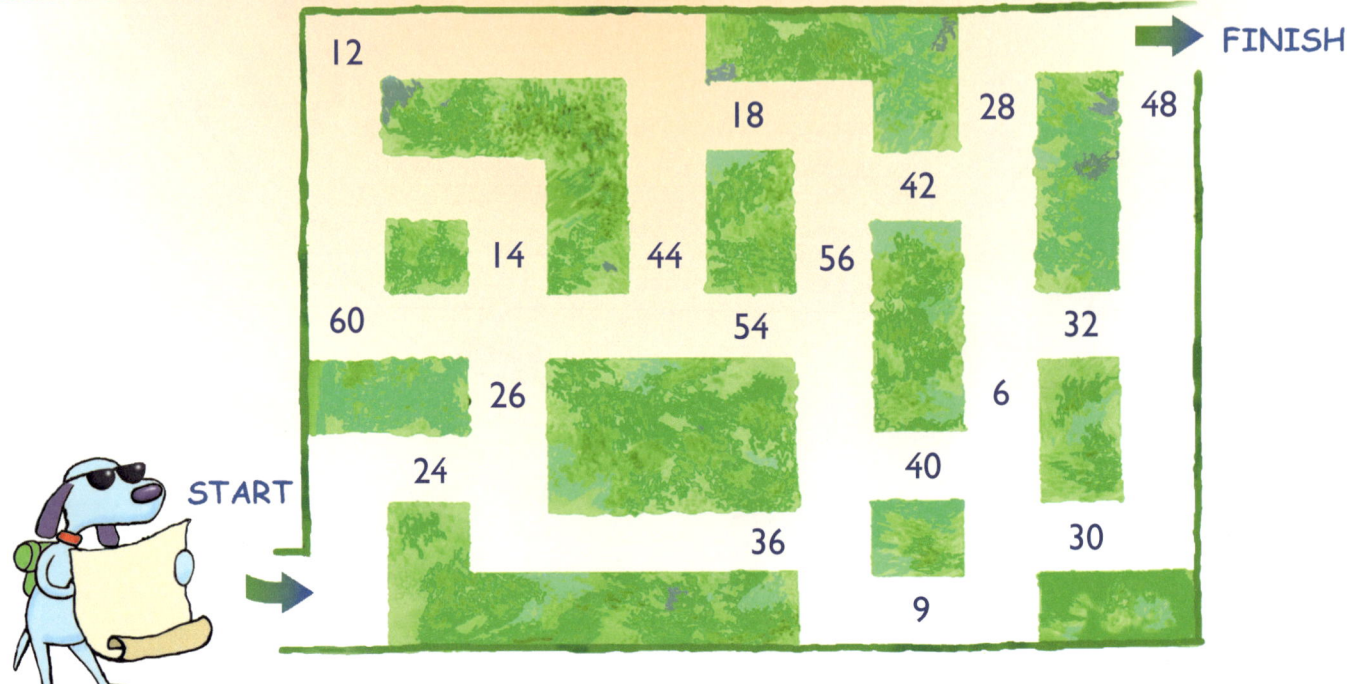

FINISH

12

18   28   48

42

14   44   56

60   54   32

26   6

24   40

START   36   30

9

Well done! Give yourself a star! ⭐

Seven Times Table

What's missing?

Fill in the missing numbers for the seven times table.

1	×	7	=	7
2	×	7	=	☐
☐	×	7	=	21
4	×	7	=	☐
5	×	7	=	35
6	×	7	=	☐
☐	×	7	=	49
8	×	7	=	☐
9	×	7	=	63
10	×	7	=	70

7   14   21   28   35   42   49

The race was on and **seven** was leading
Tripped by **fourteen** to lie knee-bleeding.
Twenty-one felled **twenty-eight**,
Who pushed him through a garden gate.
Thirty-five passed **forty-two**
Whose feet were firmly stuck with glue.
Left in the lead was **forty-nine**
With **fifty-six** quite near the line.
From far behind came **sixty-three**
But lost the race to **seventy**.

70   63   56

Let's go shopping!

A CD-Rom costs £7.

How much will it cost to buy:

5 CDs   £☐

8 CDs   £☐   How many CDs can you buy for £35? ☐

10 CDs   £☐   How many CDs can you buy for £14? ☐

9 CDs   £☐   How many CDs can you buy for £49? ☐

4 CDs   £☐   How many CDs can you buy for £21? ☐

Well done! Give yourself a star!

Calendar count

There are 7 days in one week.

Write multiplications to show the number of days for each number of weeks.

$2 \times 7 = 14$ days

☐ × ☐ = ☐ days

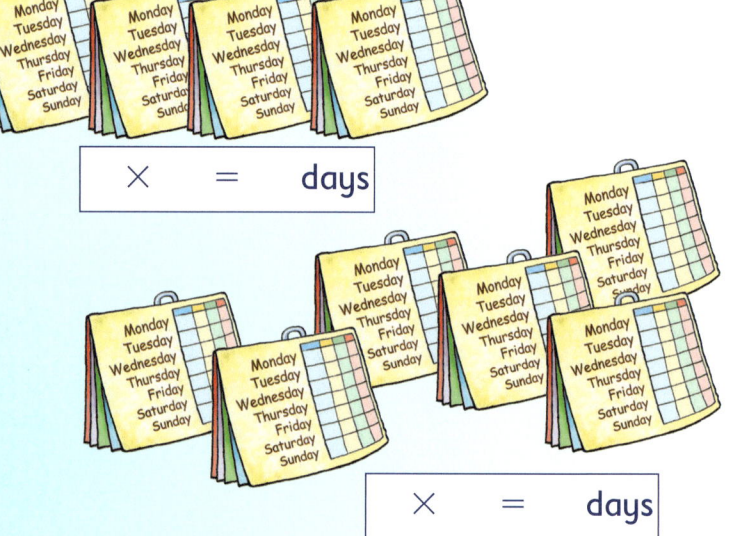

☐ × ☐ = ☐ days

☐ × ☐ = ☐ days

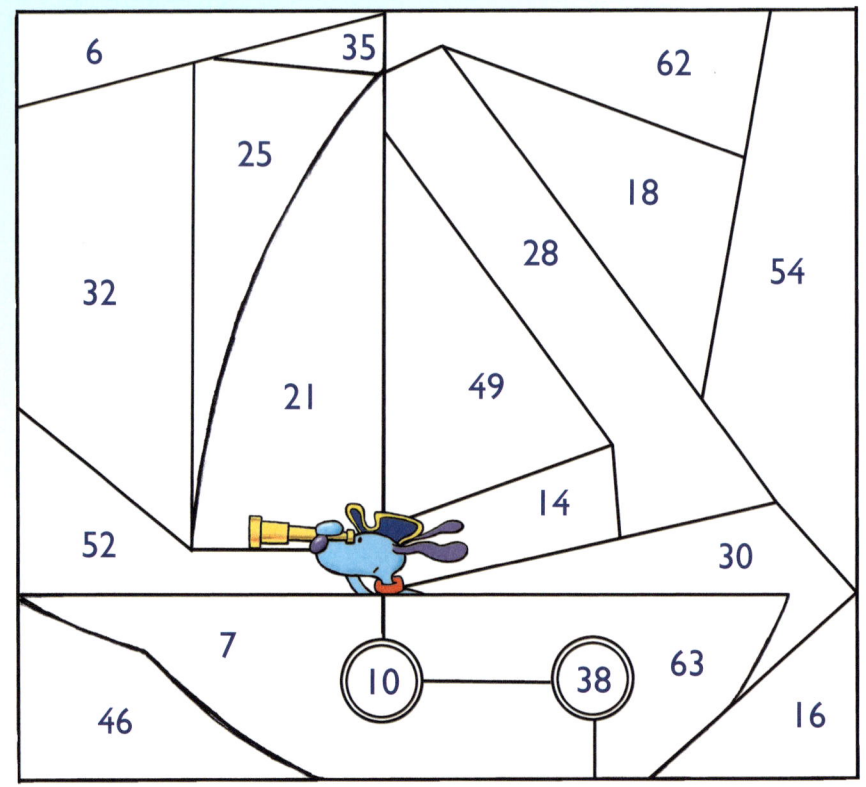

☐ × ☐ = ☐ days

Crack the code

Shade in every shape which has an answer to the seven times table.

What do you see?

```
6        35           62
     25
                  18
              28
32                      54
   21      49
              14
52                   30
   7                63
    (10)   (38)
46                     16
```

Well done! Give yourself a star!

Stepping sums!

Find a path across the river using the stepping stones.

You can only step on stones that are answers in the seven times table.

Colour the path you used.

Silly sevens!

Fill in the missing answers to these multiplications.

3 × 7 = ☐   8 × 7 = ☐   2 × 7 = ☐

9 × 7 = ☐   5 × 7 = ☐   10 × 7 = ☐

1 × 7 = ☐   6 × 7 = ☐   4 × 7 = ☐

                    7 × 7 = ☐

Well done! Give yourself a star!

Machine madness!

Here is a number machine. Each number that goes into the machine is multiplied by seven.

Fill in the missing numbers.

9 →
 → 14
 → 70
6 →
 → 35

Magic message!

Break the code to find the hidden message!

Work out the answer to the multiplication in each bubble. Then find this answer in the numbered boxes below. Write in the letter from that bubble in the space above the box. What is the hidden message?

6 × 7 **I**

1 × 7 **A**

7 × 7 **N**

2 × 7 **M**

10 × 7 **B**

9 × 7 **V**

5 × 7 **L**

8 × 7 **S**

3 × 7 **E**

4 × 7 **T**

I know my

___ ___ ___ ___ ___ ___ ___ ___ ___ ___ ___ ___ ___ ___ ___!

| 56 | 21 | 63 | 21 | 49 | 28 | 42 | 14 | 21 | 56 | 28 | 7 | 70 | 35 | 21 |

Well done! Give yourself a star!

Eight Times Table

What's missing?

Fill in the missing numbers for the eight times table.

1	×	8	=	8
2	×	☐	=	16
3	×	8	=	24
☐	×	8	=	32
5	×	8	=	☐
6	×	☐	=	48
☐	×	8	=	56
8	×	8	=	☐
9	×	8	=	72
10	×	8	=	☐

You can work out the **eight** times table if you already know the **four** times table.

Crack the code

Work out the answers to each multiplication. Then use the answers to find the correct colour in the code key.

Colour the picture.

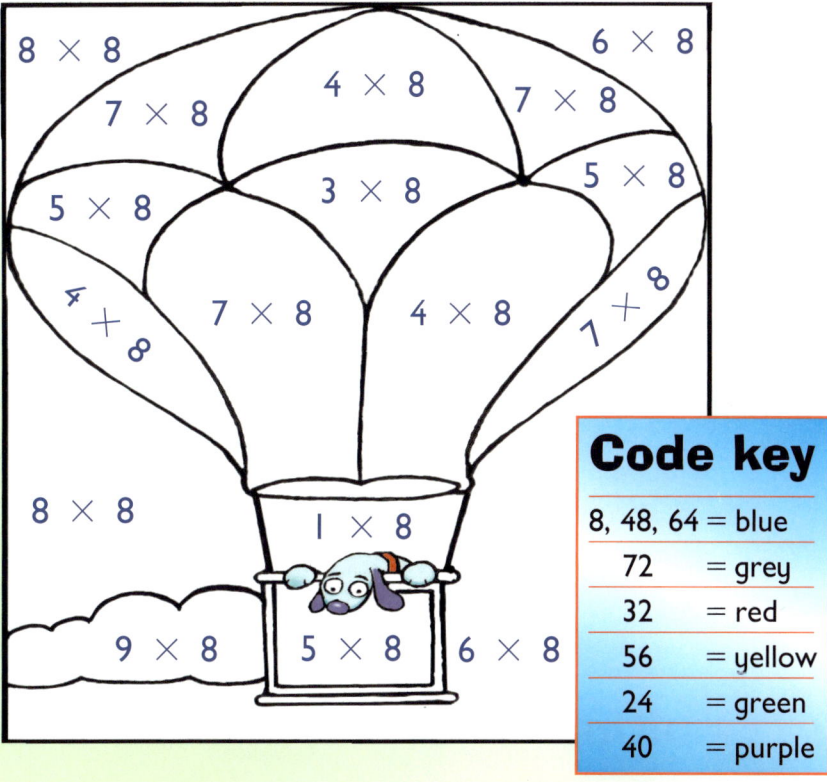

Code key

8, 48, 64	= blue
72	= grey
32	= red
56	= yellow
24	= green
40	= purple

Each answer in the **eight** times table is **double** that in the **four** times table.

1 × 4 = 4	1 × 8 = 8
2 × 4 = 8	2 × 8 = 16
3 × 4 = 12	3 × 8 = 24
4 × 4 = 16	4 × 8 = 32
5 × 4 = 20	5 × 8 = 40
6 × 4 = 24	6 × 8 = 48
7 × 4 = 28	7 × 8 = 56
8 × 4 = 32	8 × 8 = 64
9 × 4 = 36	9 × 8 = 72
10 × 4 = 40	10 × 8 = 80

Well done! Give yourself a star!

Scary spiders!

A spider has eight legs.

Write a multiplication to show the number of legs in each group of spiders.

3 × 8 = 24 legs

☐ × ☐ = ☐ legs

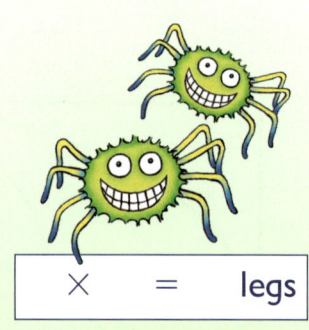

☐ × ☐ = ☐ legs

☐ × ☐ = ☐ legs

☐ × ☐ = ☐ legs

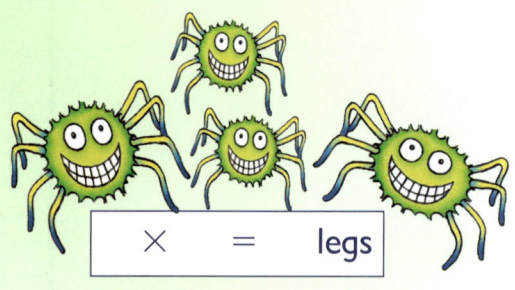

☐ × ☐ = ☐ legs

Multiplication match

Draw a line to match each multiplication to its correct answer.

4 × 8

9 × 8

2 × 8

5 × 8

7 × 8

1 × 8

32

72

16

40

56

8

Well done! Give yourself a star!

Multiplication grid

Colour all the squares that have an answer
to the eight times table.

1	2	3	4	5	6	7	8	9	10
11	12	13	14	15	16	17	18	19	20
21	22	23	24	25	26	27	28	29	30
31	32	33	34	35	36	37	38	39	40
41	42	43	44	45	46	47	48	49	50
51	52	53	54	55	56	57	58	59	60
61	62	63	64	65	66	67	68	69	70
71	72	73	74	75	76	77	78	79	80

Sea sums!

An octopus has eight legs.

How many legs do 3 octopuses have? $3 \times 8 = 24$

How many legs do 5 octopuses have?

How many legs do 6 octopuses have?

How many legs do 8 octopuses have?

There are 80 legs. How many octopuses are there?

Secret sums

Choose the correct answer for each multiplication question. Colour the letter next to that answer.

3	×	8	=	22	e	or	24	s
6	×	8	=	56	i	or	48	p
7	×	8	=	56	x	or	42	g
4	×	8	=	32	a	or	30	h
9	×	8	=	74	t	or	72	n
8	×	8	=	60	y	or	64	r

The letters that you have **not** coloured spell out the name of a number.

What is the number? [ ]

This number is the product of which multiplication in the eight times table? [ ]

Question time

Answer these questions.

1 What are four eights? [ ]

2 What is ten multiplied by eight? [ ]

3 What is 7 times 8? [ ]

4 Multiply 9 by 8. [ ]

5 Which number multiplied by 8 is 8? [ ]

6 How many eights in forty? [ ]

7 Divide 48 by 8. [ ]

8 How many eights in 24? [ ]

9 Double eight. [ ]

10 Multiply eight by itself. [ ]

Well done! Give yourself a star!

Nine Times Table

A useful way to remember the **nine times table** is to use our fingers as shown below.

What's missing?

Fill in the missing numbers for the nine times table.

1	×	9	=	9
2	×	9	=	18
3	×	9	=	☐
☐	×	9	=	36
5	×	9	=	☐
☐	×	9	=	54
7	×	9	=	63
8	×	☐	=	72
9	×	9	=	☐
10	×	9	=	90

Have you noticed that the digits in every answer in the **nine times table** add up to **9**?

A helping hand!

Complete these multiplications.

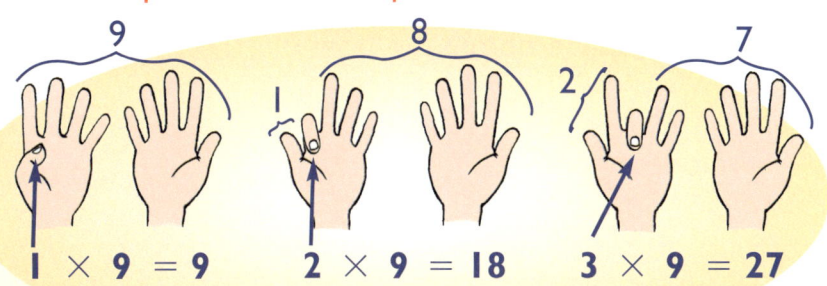

$1 \times 9 = 9$ $2 \times 9 = 18$ $3 \times 9 = 27$

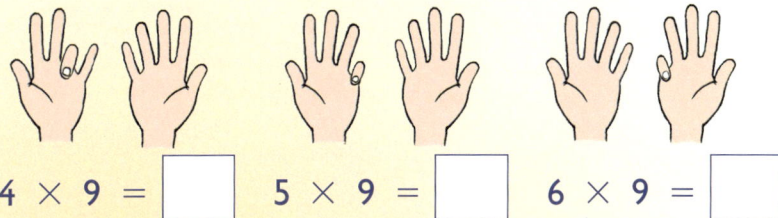

$4 \times 9 =$ ☐ $5 \times 9 =$ ☐ $6 \times 9 =$ ☐

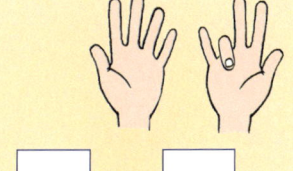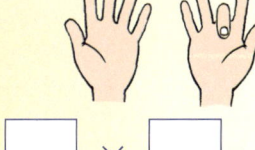

☐ × ☐ = ☐   ☐ × ☐ = ☐

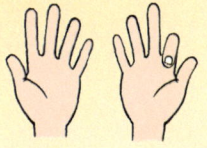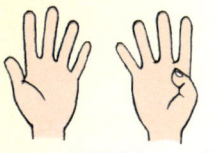

☐ × ☐ = ☐   ☐ × ☐ = ☐

9	0 + 9 = 9	
18	1 + 8 = 9	
27	2 + 7 = 9	
36	3 + 6 = 9	
45	4 + 5 = 9	
54	5 + 4 = 9	
63	6 + 3 = 9	
72	7 + 2 = 9	
81	8 + 1 = 9	
90	9 + 0 = 9	

Well done! Give yourself a star!

Magic message!

Break the code to find the hidden word.

Work out the answer to the multiplication in each bubble. Then find this answer in the numbered boxes below. Write in the letter from that bubble in the space above the box.

What is the hidden word?

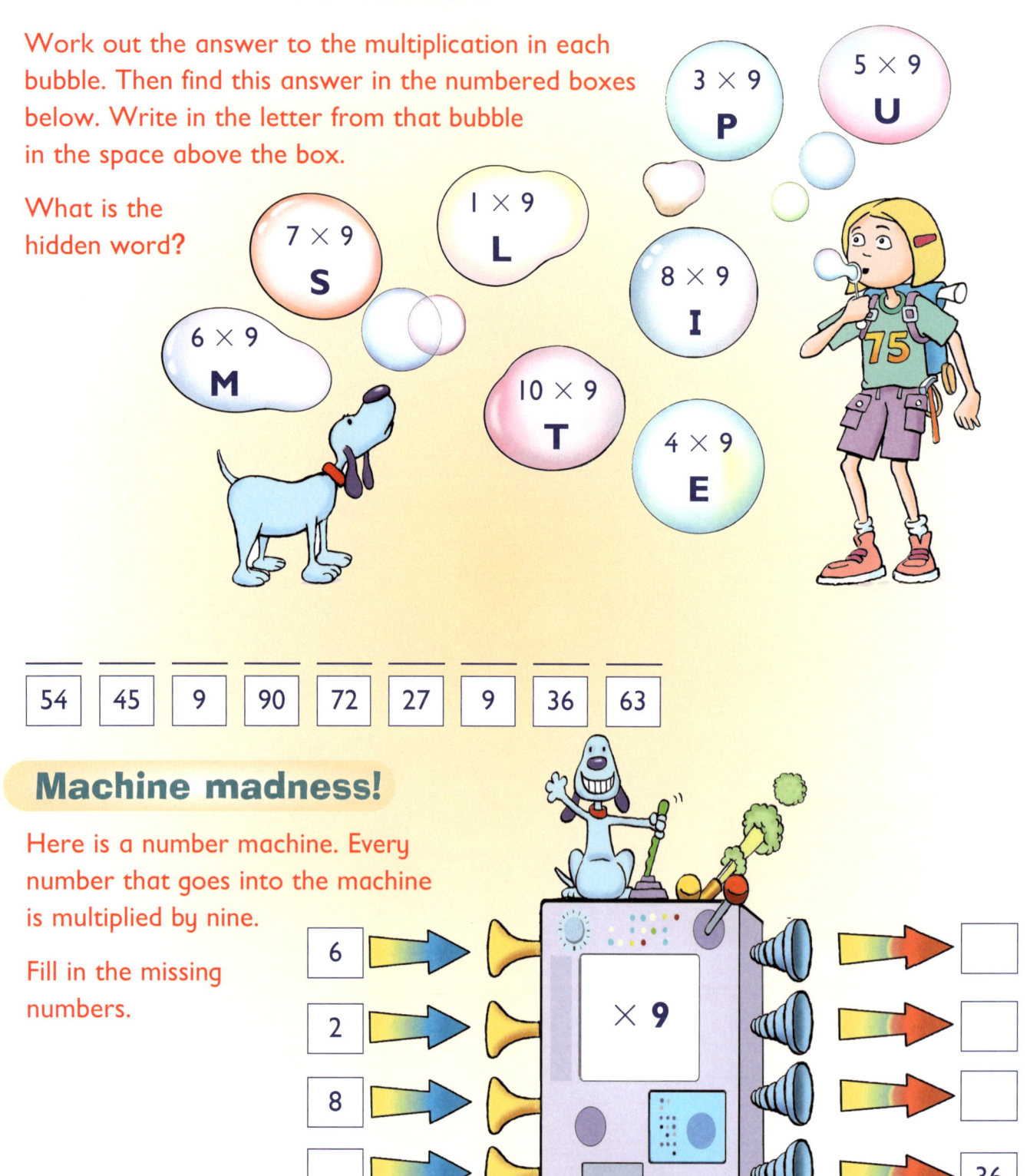

3×9 — P

5×9 — U

1×9 — L

7×9 — S

8×9 — I

6×9 — M

10×9 — T

4×9 — E

54	45	9	90	72	27	9	36	63

Machine madness!

Here is a number machine. Every number that goes into the machine is multiplied by nine.

Fill in the missing numbers.

× 9

6 → □
2 → □
8 → □
□ → 36
□ → 90

Well done! Give yourself a star!

Naughty nines!

Fill in the missing numbers to complete
these multiplications.

36	=	☐	×	9		45	=	☐	×	9
90	=	☐	×	9		72	=	☐	×	9
9	=	☐	×	9		27	=	☐	×	9
18	=	☐	×	9		63	=	☐	×	9
54	=	☐	×	9						

Multiplication maze

Find a path through the maze. You can only
go through numbers which are answers in the
nine times table.

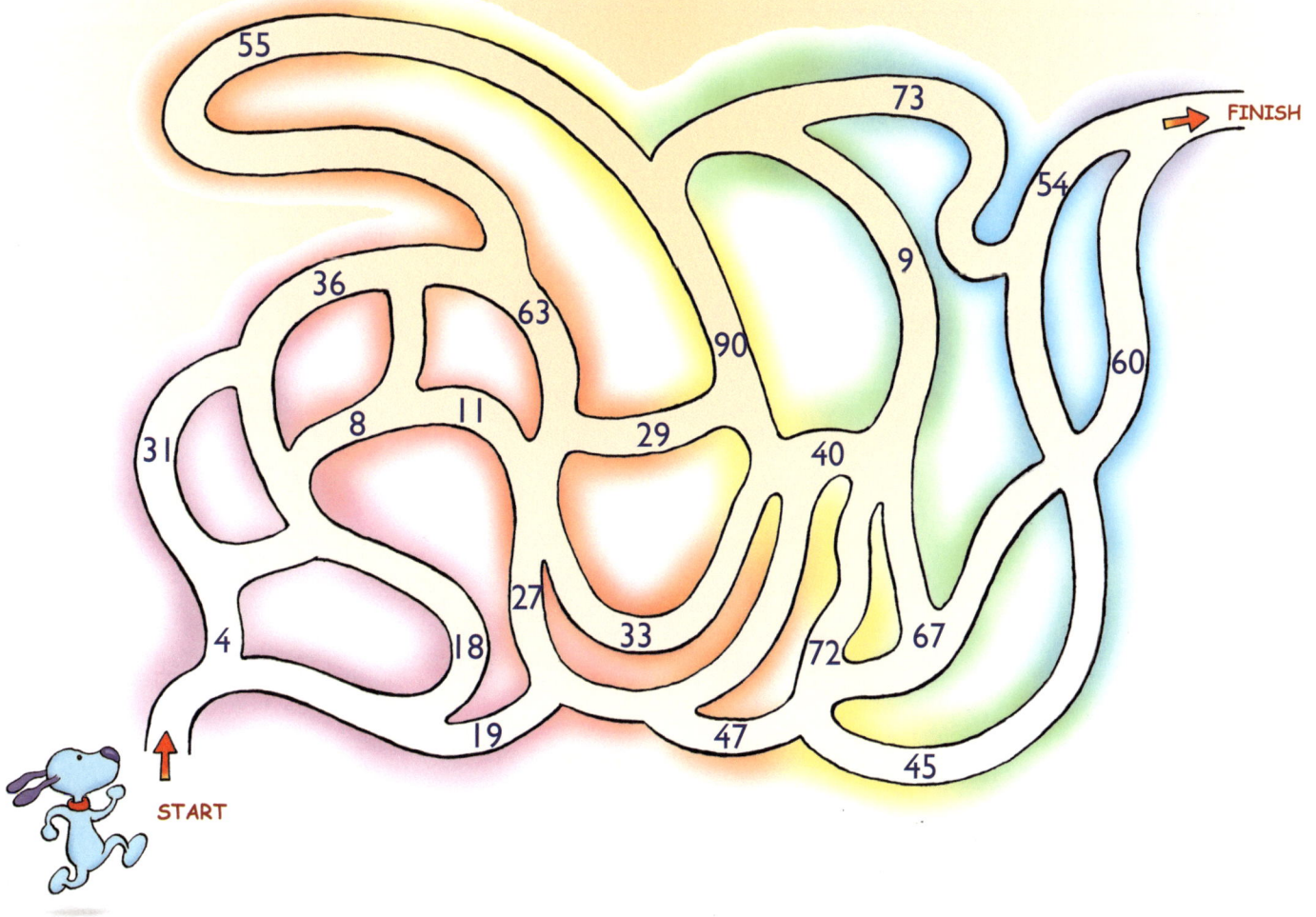

Well done! Give yourself a star!

Crack the code!

Work out the answers to each multiplication. Then use the answers to find the correct colour in the code key.

Colour the picture.

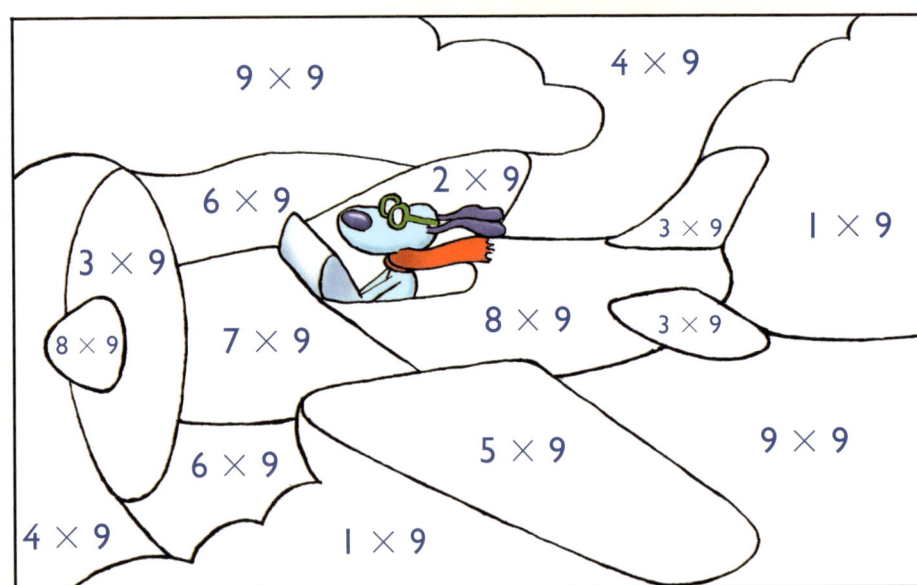

Code key

9, 81	=	dark blue
18, 45	=	light green
27	=	yellow
63, 72	=	dark green
36, 54	=	light blue

Question time!

Answer the questions.

1 What is 9×9?

2 What is the fourth multiple of nine?

3 What is three times nine?

4 The sixth multiple of nine is 45.
Is this true or false?

5 What is the product of 7 and 9?

6 How many nines are in 90?

7 A pencil costs 9p. I have 45p.
How many pencils can I buy?

8 Double 9.

9 What is eight multiplied by nine?

If you write down the **multiples of nine** in a column you will see a pattern which makes it easy to remember them.

0	9
1	8
2	7
3	6
4	5
5	4
6	3
7	2
8	1
9	0

Well done! Give yourself a star!

Mixed Tables

Machine madness!

Here are some number machines. Fill in the missing number on the machine.

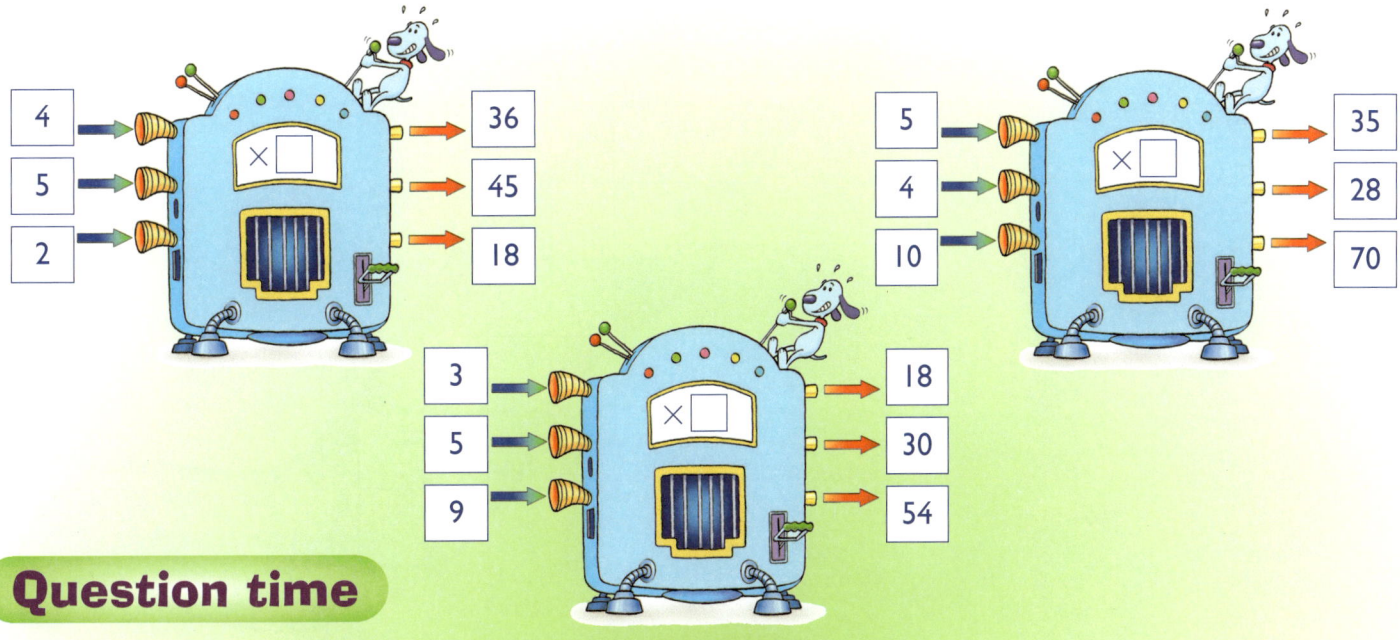

Question time

Answer these questions.

1 What is the product of 6 and 7?

2 Which number multiplied by itself gives the answer 49?

3 What is the sixth multiple of 6?

4 What do you need to multiply 9 by to get 45?

5 What is 32 divided by 4?

6 How many sevens in 56?

7 The multiplications 3 × 8 and 8 × 3 both give the product 24. ☐ and ☐
Which other two multiplications give the product 24?

8 Find two different multiplications which give the product 30. ☐ and ☐

9 What is the eighth multiple of 8?

10 What number multiplied by itself gives 81?

Well done! Give yourself a star!

Snakey sums

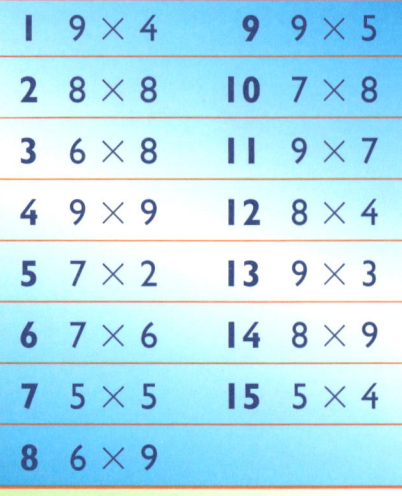

1	9 × 4	9	9 × 5
2	8 × 8	10	7 × 8
3	6 × 8	11	9 × 7
4	9 × 9	12	8 × 4
5	7 × 2	13	9 × 3
6	7 × 6	14	8 × 9
7	5 × 5	15	5 × 4
8	6 × 9		

Snake grid cells: 1 → 3, 2 → 6, 3 → 4, 4, 5, 6, 7, 8, 9, 10, 11, 12, 13, 14, 15, 16

This is a zig-zag multiplication snake.

Work out each multiplication and write the answer in the grid.

The last digit of each answer is the first digit of the next answer.

The first two have been filled in for you.

Forward and back

Count on and back for each of the times tables.

3		9			18		24		30
40				24	20		12		4
5			20	25			40		50
60	54								6
7		21		35		49		63	70
80	72		56				24		8
9			36			63			90
100		80		60		40			10

Well done! Give yourself a star!

Circling sums

Look at the numbers below.

7	49	32		70
			24	
42	48	21		
				16
	56		40	
6	30	63		

Circle in **red** the multiples of 7.
Circle in **orange** the multiples of 8.

Which number have you circled twice?

Multiplication monster!

A multi-monster has **three** heads, **six** eyes, **nine** ears and **four** arms.

How many heads, eyes, ears and arms are there on:

3 multi-monsters?

☐ heads   ☐ eyes
☐ ears   ☐ arms

10 multi-monsters?

☐ heads   ☐ eyes
☐ ears   ☐ arms

7 multi-monsters?

☐ heads   ☐ eyes
☐ ears   ☐ arms

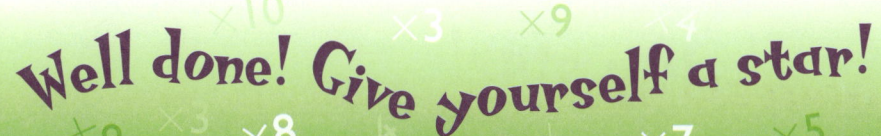

Well done! Give yourself a star! ★

Daring darts!

Here are some targets.

If an arrow lands in the outer-most ring it scores 2 times (double) the number.

If it lands in the middle ring it scores 3 times (treble) the number.

If it lands in the inner-most ring it scores 10 times the number.

Write down the score for each target.

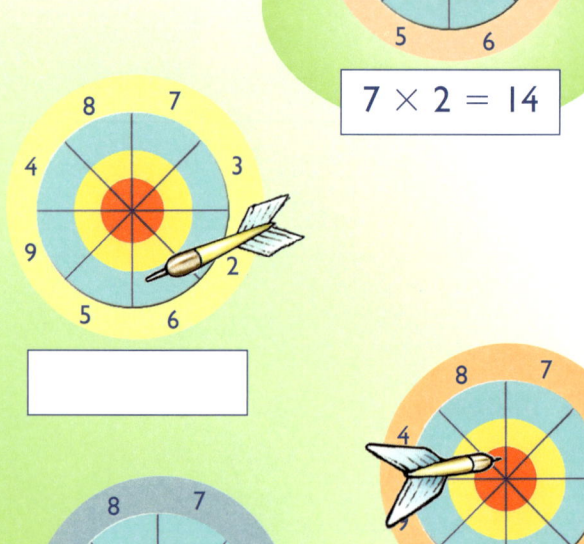

$7 \times 2 = 14$

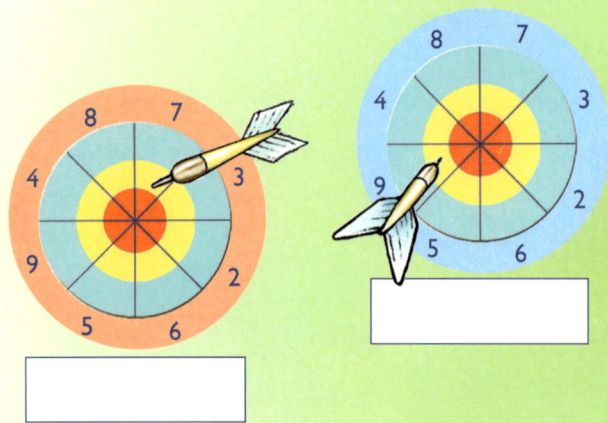

Multiplication match

Match each product to its correct answer.

7×7

6×7

8×8

8×6

8×9

9×7

49

42

72

48

63

64

Well done! Give yourself a star!

Let's go shopping!

Here are some items for sale in the toy shop.

How much would it cost to buy:

two skateboards £ ☐   five pencils ☐ p

six books £ ☐   eight yo-yos ☐ p

four footballs £ ☐   ten rubbers ☐ p

seven trains £ ☐   nine badges ☐ p

How many pencils could you buy for 49p? ☐

How many trains could you buy for £36? ☐

How many books could you buy for £27? ☐

Multiplication mix!

Fill in the answers to these multiplications.

$3 \times 6 =$ ☐ $4 \times 7 =$ ☐ $5 \times 8 =$ ☐

$2 \times 9 =$ ☐ $3 \times 10 =$ ☐ $4 \times 4 =$ ☐

$7 \times 6 =$ ☐ $6 \times 8 =$ ☐ $9 \times 7 =$ ☐

$8 \times 8 =$ ☐ $7 \times 2 =$ ☐ $10 \times 9 =$ ☐

$5 \times 4 =$ ☐ $9 \times 3 =$ ☐ $4 \times 8 =$ ☐

Well done! Give yourself a star!

Multiplication mayhem!

Here's a real challenge. Complete the full multiplication grid!

x	1	2	3	4	5	6	7	8	9	10
1	1	2								
2		4								
3				12						
4								32		
5			15							
6						36				
7										70
8							56			
9									81	
10					50					

Magic message!

Break the code to find the hidden message!

Work out the answer to the multiplication in each bubble. Then find this answer in the numbered boxes below. Write in the letter from that bubble in the space above the box.

What is the hidden message?

4 × 6 **A**

9 × 4 **V**

7 × 4 **F**

6 × 3 **I**

6 × 9 **E**

5 × 7 **S**

2 × 10 **D**

3 × 5 **H**

8 × 7 **N**

___ ___ ___ ___ ___   ___ ___ ___ ___ ___ ___ ___ ___ !

18		15	24	36	54		28	18	56	18	35	15	54	20

Well done! Give yourself a star!

Answers

Three Times Table

Page 3   **Can you remember?**
3, 6, 9, 12, 15, 18, 21, 24, 27, 30
Multiplication maze
Follow a path through the numbers: 6, 18, 30, 12, 15, 24, 27, 3, 21
Buying books
12, 6; 15, 24; 30, 21; 6 books

Page 4   **Multiplication match**
Circle: 10 × 3; 7 × 3; 5 × 3; 8 × 3
Machine madness!
3, 8, 1, 6

Four Times Table

Page 5   **Can you remember?**
4, 8, 12, 16, 20, 24, 28, 32, 36, 40
Secret shapes
Colour: 4, 28, 24, 8, 40, 20, 12, 36, 16
It's a stakeboarder!
Fairground fun!
20, 12; 28, 8; 24, 40; 4 tickets

Page 6   **Machine madness!**
Double/Double machine: 8, 16, 28;
× 4 machine: 8, 16, 28
These number machines produce the same numbers. *Note to parent: Your child should recognise that doubling a number twice is the same as multiplying a number by four.*
Number path
Follow a path through the numbers: 16, 12, 24, 28, 32, 40, 36, 8, 4, 20

Mixed Tables

Page 7   **Money multiplication**
2 × 2p = 4p; 1 × 2p = 2p; 6 × 5p = 30p;
3 × 10p = 30p; 7 × 10p = 70p;
Circling sums
The numbers 10 and 20 have three different coloured rings around them.
The numbers 3 and 11 do not have any rings around them. *Note to parent: Your child should recognise that the numbers 10 and 20 are answers in the two, five and ten times tables.*

Page 8   **Machine madness!**
×2/×5 machine: 30, 50, 80;
×10 machine: 30, 50, 80
These number machines produce the same numbers. *Note to parent: Your child should recognise that multiplying a number by 2 and then 5 is the same as multiplying a number by 10.*
Multiplication mix
8, 14, 16; 25, 15, 45; 50, 10, 100; 10, 18, 80

Six Times Table

Page 9   **What's missing?**
18, 4, 36, 7, 54
Let's go shopping!
18, 24, 42, 6, 48

Page 10   **Mysterious match!**
Match: 4 × 6 – 24; 9 × 6 – 54;
3 × 6 – 18; 10 × 6 – 60; 2 × 6 – 12;
7 × 6 – 42
Machine madness!
36, 3, 1, 54, 4

Page 11   **Sums for sixes**
8, 4; 7, 10; 1, 2; 3, 6; 9, 5
Tricky treasure!
5 × 6 = 30; 6 × 6 = 36; 7 × 6 = 42;
4 × 6 = 24; 2 × 6 = 12

Page 12   **Secret sums**
Shade in the letters: s, i, n, r, a, m
The number is **twelve**; twelve is the product of **2 × 6**.
Number path
Follow a path through the numbers: 24, 36, 54, 60, 12, 18, 42, 6, 30, 48

Seven Times Table

Page 13   **What's missing?**
14, 3, 28, 42, 7, 56
Let's go shopping!
35; 56, 5 CDs; 70, 2 CDs; 63, 7 CDs; 28, 3 CDs

Page 14   **Calendar count**
3 × 7 = 21 days; **4 × 7 = 28** days;
5 × 7 = 35 days; **6 × 7 = 42** days
Crack the code
Colour the numbers: 35, 21, 49, 28, 14, 7, 63
It's a yacht!

Page 15   **Stepping sums!**
Colour: 35, 14, 49, 56, 70, 7, 21, 42
Silly sevens!
21, 56, 14; 63, 35, 70; 7, 42, 28; 49

Page 16   **Machine madness!**
63, 2, 10, 42, 5
Magic message!
I know my **SEVEN TIMES TABLE**!

Eight Times Table

Page 17   **What's missing?**
8, 4, 40, 8, 7, 64, 80

Crack the code
Colour: 8×8 – blue; 7×8 – yellow;
4×8 – red; 7×8 – yellow; 6×8 – blue;
5×8 – purple; 3×8 – green;
5×8 – purple; 4×8 – red;
7×8 – yellow; 4×8 – red;
7×8 – yellow; 8×8 – blue; 1×8 blue;
9×8 – grey; 5×8 – purple; 6×8 – blue

Page 18   **Scary spiders!**
$5 \times 8 = \mathbf{40}$ legs; $2 \times 8 = \mathbf{16}$ legs;
$8 \times 8 = \mathbf{64}$ legs; $6 \times 8 = \mathbf{48}$ legs;
$4 \times 8 = \mathbf{32}$ legs
Multiplication match
Match: $4 \times 8 – 32$; $9 \times 8 – 72$;
$2 \times 8 – 16$; $5 \times 8 – 40$; $7 \times 8 – 56$;
$1 \times 8 – 8$

Page 19   **Multiplication grid**
Colour the squares numbered: 8, 16, 24, 32,
40, 48, 56, 64, 72, 80
Sea sums!
$5 \times 8 = 40$; $6 \times 8 = 48$; $8 \times 8 = 64$;
10 octopuses

Page 20   **Secret sums**
Shade in the letters: s, p, x, a, n, r
The number is **eighty**; eighty is the product
of $\mathbf{10 \times 8}$.
Question time
1 32 **2** 80 **3** 56 **4** 72 **5** 1 **6** 5 **7** 6 **8** 3
9 16 **10** 64

Nine Times Table

Page 21   **What's missing?**
27, 4, 45, 6, 9, 81
A helping hand!
$4 \times 9 = \mathbf{36}$; $5 \times 9 = \mathbf{45}$; $6 \times 9 = \mathbf{54}$;
$7 \times 9 = \mathbf{63}$; $8 \times 9 = \mathbf{72}$; $9 \times 9 = \mathbf{81}$;
$10 \times 9 = \mathbf{90}$

Page 22   **Magic message!**
MULTIPLES
Machine madness!
54, 18, 72, 4, 10

Page 23   **Naughty nines!**
$36 = \mathbf{4} \times 9$; $45 = \mathbf{5} \times 9$; $90 = \mathbf{10} \times 9$;
$72 = \mathbf{8} \times 9$; $9 = \mathbf{1} \times 9$; $27 = \mathbf{3} \times 9$;
$18 = \mathbf{2} \times 9$; $63 = \mathbf{7} \times 9$; $54 = \mathbf{6} \times 9$
Multiplication maze
Follow a path through the numbers: 18, 36,
63, 27, 90, 9, 72, 45, 54

Page 23   **Crack the code!**
Colour: 9×9 – dark blue; 4×9 – light blue;
1×9 – dark blue; 4×9 – light blue;
8×9 – dark green; 3×9 – yellow;
6×9 – light blue; 2×9 – light green;
3×9 – yellow; 7×9 – dark green;
8×9 – dark green; 3×9 – yellow;
6×9 – light blue; 1×9 – dark blue;
5×9 – light green; 9×9 – dark blue;

Question time!
1 81 **2** 36 **3** 27 **4** false, it's 54 **5** 63 **6** 10
7 5 pencils **8** 18 **9** 72

Mixed Tables

Page 25   **Machine madness!**
$\times 8$, $\times 9$, $\times 6$, $\times 7$
Question time
1 42 **2** 7 **3** 36 **4** 5 **5** 8 **6** 8 **7** 6 x 4 and
4 x 6 **8** Either 3×10, 10×3, 6×5
or 5×6 **9** 64 **10** 9

Page 26   **Snakey sums**
1 36 **2** 64 **3** 48 **4** 81 **5** 14 **6** 42 **7** 25
8 54 **9** 45 **10** 56 **11** 63 **12** 32 **13** 27
14 72 **15** 20
Forward and back
6, 12, 15, 21, 27; 36, 32, 28, 16, 8; 10, 15,
30, 35, 45; 48, 42, 36, 30, 24, 18, 12; 14, 28,
42, 56; 64, 48, 40, 32, 16; 18, 27, 45, 54, 72,
81; 90, 70, 50, 30, 20

Page 27   **Circling sums**
56 *Note to parent: Your child should recognise
that the number 56 is an answer in the seven
and eight times tables.*
Multiplication monster
3 multi-monsters: 9 heads, 18 eyes;
27 ears, 12 arms
10 multi-monsters: 30 heads, 60 eyes;
90 ears, 40 arms
7 multi-monsters: 21 heads, 42 eyes;
54 ears, 28 arms

Page 28   **Daring darts!**
$6 \times 2 = 12$; $7 \times 3 = 21$; $9 \times 3 = 27$;
$6 \times 10 = 60$; $8 \times 10 = 80$
Multiplication match
Match: $7 \times 7 = 49$; $6 \times 7 = 42$;
$8 \times 8 = 64$; $8 \times 6 = 48$; $8 \times 9 = 72$;
$9 \times 7 = 63$

Page 29   **Let's go shopping!**
18, 35; 18, 80; 8, 40; 42, 72; 7 pencils; 6
trains; 9 books
Multiplication mix!
18, 28, 40; 18, 30, 16; 42, 48, 63; 64, 14, 90;
20, 27, 32

Page 30   **Multiplication mayhem!**

x	1	2	3	4	5	6	7	8	9	10
1	1	2	3	4	5	6	7	8	9	10
2	2	4	6	8	10	12	14	16	18	20
3	3	6	9	12	15	18	21	24	27	30
4	4	8	12	16	20	24	28	32	36	40
5	5	10	15	20	25	30	35	40	45	50
6	6	12	18	24	30	36	42	48	54	60
7	7	14	21	28	35	42	49	56	63	70
8	8	16	24	32	40	48	56	64	72	80
9	9	18	27	36	45	54	63	72	81	90
10	10	20	30	04	50	60	70	80	90	100

Magic message!
I HAVE FINISHED!